# Mind-Sharpening Logic Games

Andrea Angiolino

Sterling Publishing Co., Inc.
New York

To all the friends of "The Louis,"
adventurous student magazine


*Drawings by Sandro Zack*
*Computer illustrations by Andrea Angiolino*


10 9 8 7 6 5 4 3 2 1

Published in 2003 by Sterling Publishing Company, Inc.
387 Park Avenue South, New York, NY 10016
©1995 by Sterling Publishing Co., Inc.
Originally published under the title *Super Sharp Pencil & Paper Games*
Distributed in Canada by Sterling Publishing
c/o Canadian Manda Group, One Atlantic Avenue, Suite 105
Toronto, Ontario, Canada M6K 3E7
Distributed in Great Britain and Europe by Chrysalis Books
64 Brewery Road, London N7 9NT England
Distributed in Australia by Capricorn Link (Australia) Pty. Ltd.
P.O. Box 704, Windsor, NSW 2756 Australia

Sterling ISBN 1-4027-0412-7

# Contents

# Introduction

People enjoy all kinds of games: technological games that require sophisticated computers, science-fiction machinery with virtual reality, and games played with paper and pencil, with a stone, or with nothing at all. We have learned some of these games from our friends and relatives; others we learn after buying them.

This book includes thirty-eight games you can play with only pencil and paper. We will talk about games that are less well known as well as some that are better known. You probably already know some of the traditional games, such as *The Track* and *Nim*. We like to talk about them because people usually learn these games orally, and this is a good opportunity to put them on paper, formalizing the rules.

All the games we've included have very simple rules. You can learn them in a maximum of a minute and remember them easily. However, the strategy and the winning tactics are not as easy and apparent. If children can have fun playing *Hex* or *Black* without too much effort, adolescents and adults who decide to apply themselves will discover almost inexhaustible possibilities. In some cases, we have been able to present some curious variations that can add to the players' enthusiasm for repeated playing.

The second part of the book consists of pointers about a few of the games. Some of these ideas may be hard for the youngest readers to follow, but you don't need these discussions to play the games. For those who are interested, these observations on strategy will lead to some fascinating conclusions.

Furthermore, studying these games is like assembling a train set. You can learn a lot by examining the mechanism of the engine, and that can be as enjoyable as running it on the tracks. However, the point of any game is to play. Without analyzing them too much, the games in this book are very educational. You need all sorts of knowledge to play: language, mathematics, geometry, logic, and an understanding of the binary system.

This book is a tool for exercising the mind. All of us, big and small, can enjoy this kind of exercise. You can play these games while riding a bus, waiting in line at the post office, or in the waiting room at the dentist's. You only need a pencil, a piece of paper, and an opponent to challenge. May the best player win!

## PART ONE
# LET'S START PLAYING RIGHT AWAY!

*"These rules are so simple that a
four-year-old could understand them.
Chico, go find me a four-year-old because I
can't understand anything."*
(Groucho Marx)

# The Walls

**Players:** Two

**Supplies:** Paper and pencil

**Rules:** Start by drawing a continuous, winding line. Divide it into different regions. To do this, both players take turns drawing a line, until they create twenty to thirty regions, as shown in the drawing on the left.

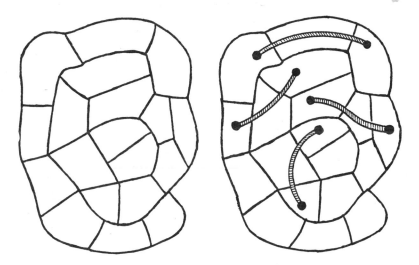

Now, the game starts. The players *take turns* drawing a "Chinese Wall" that starts in a region, crosses an adjacent region, and ends in a third region, as shown in the drawing on the right. The first player who cannot do this loses.

# Black

*William Black invented this game.*

**Players:** Two

**Supplies:** Graph paper and pencil

**Rules:** Draw a 6✕6 playing board.

The first player selects one of the three symbols shown above, representing the curves and intersections of a road. The player draws it in the top left-hand square of the board. The second player selects any one of the three symbols and draws it in an adjacent square, continuing the road begun by the first player.

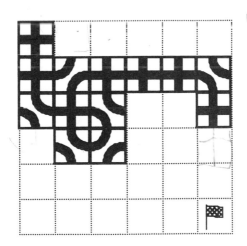

Notice that in the squares with intersections, the road enters on one side and must exit on exactly the opposite side.

The player who draws a symbol in the bottom right-hand square wins the game.

A player loses if he forces the road to end at the edge of the paper, preventing the other player from making his next move.

In the example shown here, the player must move in the top right-hand square. He can choose any of the three symbols, but the road will end at the edge of the paper, and he will lose the game.

**Variations:** The dimensions of the playing board can vary, although it is advisable to keep each side five to eight squares in length.

# Mishmash

*Rev. Charles Lutwidge Dodgson invented* Mishmash *in 1882. Also known as Lewis Carroll, Dodgson is the author of* The Dynamics of a Particle, Euclid and His Modern Rivals, The Hunting of the Snark, Logic Games, *and* Alice's Adventures in Wonderland.
Mishmash *was also the name of one of the newspapers that Carroll prepared for relatives and friends. He "published" it from 1853 to 1862.*

**Players:** Two

**Supplies:** Paper and pencil

**Rules:** Each player picks a small block of two or more letters called a "core." When each player has selected a core, the players tell each other their cores.

Each player must then find a word that contains the opponent's selected core. Players may not use proper nouns.

For example, Laura writes CROS while Ernest writes FUL. They tell each other their choices. Laura can use the word PLAY-FUL-NESS and Ernest can use A-CROS-S or A-CROS-TIC, but he can't use CROS-S because the core must not be at the end or beginning of the word.

The first player who finds an appropriate word, decides that an appropriate word doesn't exist, or gives up says, "Done," "It doesn't exist," or "I give up." At this point, the opponent has two minutes to finish.

If the first player has said, "Done," he must now announce the word he found. If he said, "It doesn't exist," his opponent can immediately state a word containing his core.

Then the second player has to announce a word that contains his own core, or the first player must suggest a word.

A player earns one point by finding an appropriate word. If he says he has found it, but the word is incorrect, he loses one point, and the other player wins one point.

If the first player says, "It doesn't exist," and his opponent can't find a word for him, the first player wins two points. If the opponent can find it, the first player loses two points to him. If the first player says, "I give up," he loses one point and his opponent gains one point.

For on each turn, the players propose a new core, unless a player fails to respond or says, "I'm not done," in which case he continues to play with the same core from the last round.

When a player says, "I give up," the players discard that core for the remainder of the game. When this happens, it is possible to propose very similar cores, differing by only one letter. For example, in one round the first player could suggest GRAL, and when the players discard GRAL, the first player could pick AGRAL for the next round, even though it contains the same set of letters.

The first player to reach ten points wins.

Even if these rules seem hard, don't get discouraged. Try to play. This game is much easier than it sounds.

# Mine Field

Mine Field *is a simple, almost childish game. The "Sturmtruppen" (Storm Troopers) were German assault troops during World War II. In 1979, Giorgio Corbetta and Mario Gomboli published* Paper and Pencil Battles with the Sturmtruppen, *a book of paper and pencil games that included this game. They called it* Mine Field *because the game, with its imaginary explosions, helps people realize that it is better to play, without real mines and war.*

**Players:** Two players

**Supplies:** Paper and pencil

**Rules:** Each player privately prepares two 7 × 9 playing boards. The side with seven squares is numbered from 1 to 7. On one of the two boards, the player places ten "mines," drawing a point at the intersection of the squares. No player can have more than two mines on the same line, horizontally or vertically. Players may not place mines on the start or end points.

Taking turns, the players advance by drawing a line, announcing a direction, and moving a square horizontally, vertically, or diagonally. When a player hits a mine, he stays where he is.

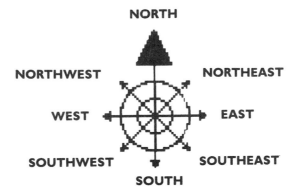

Clockwise, the eight directions are: north, northeast, east, southeast, south, southwest, west, and northwest as shown in the drawing above.

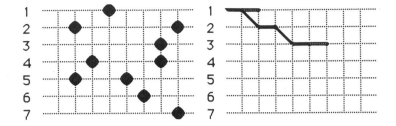

For example, on the left in the drawing above, we have the hidden mines that Olivia placed. On the right, we see her attempt to cross Carl's mine field. Olivia started by saying, "I start in 1 and go to the east." Because there were no mines, she could draw her line. The second time she tried east, there was a mine, and she stayed on the same line. The third time, she moved southeast; the fourth, east; the fifth, southeast; the sixth, east; and the seventh, she tried east, but there was a mine, forcing her to stay at the same point.

The object is to cross the mine field from left to right. If the second player succeeds, he wins. If his opponent succeeds, the second player has the right to a final move, so that both players have the same number of attempts. If the second player reaches the right side of the field on this last turn, the game ends in a tie. If not, the first player wins.

# Hex

In 1942, the Danish mathematician Piet Hein presented the game now called Hex during a lecture to his students at the Copenhagen Institute of Theoretical Physics. For those who think this wasn't the right place to introduce a game, here's a poem by Piet Hein himself:

> "Considering the game as a simple game,
> the practice will demonstrate all too clearly
> how much both players
> have scarcely understood."

Danes call this game Polygon. Americans call it John or Nash because John Nash, an expert in games theory, introduced it to the United States. He played it on the hexagonal tiles of the bathroom at his university. Parker Brothers created the name Hex when they produced it in a box version in 1952.

**Players:** Two

**Supplies:** Paper and pencil

**Rules:** The game uses an 11×11 playing board made up of hexagons, as shown in the drawing below.

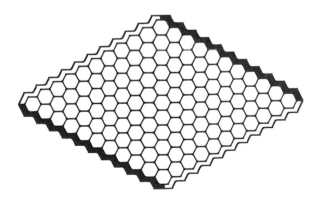

Because the players have to draw it themselves, it may be easier to use squares instead of hexagons, like the ones in the drawing below.

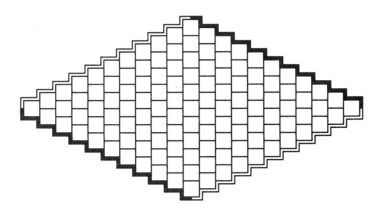

One player is White, and the other is Black. Each player takes one side of the board. The corner squares belong to both players.

The players take turns, drawing one circle of their respective colors in a blank square each turn. The object is to connect both sides of the board with an uninterrupted chain of circles of the same colors. In the drawing below, for instance, black has won.

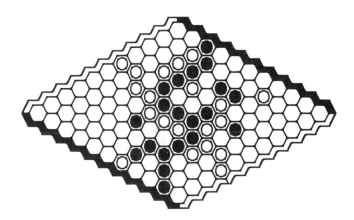

**Variations:** To balance the game, which normally favors the first player, theorists have proposed several solutions:

- The players play two rounds of the game, changing sides. If a player wins both rounds, he wins the game. If each player wins one round, the winner is the one who won his round with the fewest number of moves.
- A player cannot make his first move on the central column of squares shown in gray in the drawing below.

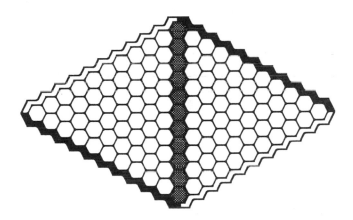

- The first player draws one circle the first move, and then both players draw two circles per turn.

# Brigitte

Brigitte *is a relative of* Hex, *played on a board prepared as shown in the drawing on the left. David Gale invented it. Some people call it* Gale, *but others call it* Bird Cage.

**Players:** Two

**Supplies:** Paper and pencil

**Rules:** Prepare a board, as in the drawing below.

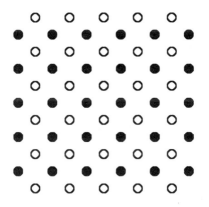

One player is Black, and the other is White. Taking turns, the players connect pairs of adjacent dots of their color with a horizontal or vertical line. The only restriction is that a player cannot cross the lines made by his adversary. To win, Black must connect the right and left sides of the board with an uninterrupted chain of dashes, and White must connect the top and bottom sides.

The drawing below represents a game won by Black.

The dimensions of the board can vary. Usually it is better not to use a smaller board than the one shown in the figure.

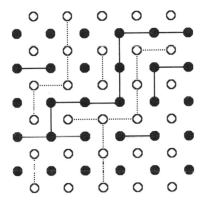

**Variations:** The name *Brigitte* comes from *Bridge-it*, which was the name of a box version of the game sold in the United States. In this variation, the players have a limited number of plastic strips used to connect the dots. Once they run out, they must reuse one of the strips already played.

*Twixt* is another relative of *Brigitte*. Invented by Alex Randolph in 1962, *Twixt* is a box game.

# Scaffold

Scaffold, *a traditional game, is a poor cousin of* Brigitte.

**Players:** Two

**Supplies** Graph paper and two pencils of different colors.

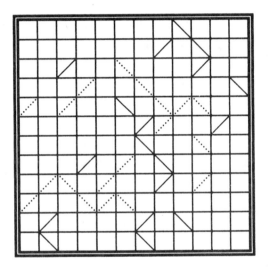

**Rules:** Draw a 12×12 playing board.

Taking turns, each player draws a diagonal line through a square with his colored pencil. Players may not draw a diagonal line through a square that either player has already used. A player's diagonal line may not touch the end of a diagonal made by his opponent. The object of the first player is to connect the right and left sides of the board with a chain of diagonals. The second player must connect the top and bottom sides of the board. The first to do so wins.

# The Francoprussian Labyrinth

*As described in mythology, the labyrinth was a huge and intricate structure made by the king of Crete to hide the Minotaur, a creature half human and half bull that ate boys and girls. The hero Theseus was able to walk through the labyrinth and kill the monster.*

*In this game, we pretend to be Theseus hunting the beast.*

**Players:** Two

**Supplies:** Graph paper and pencil

**Rules:** Each player draws two 9×9 playing boards.

A player uses one to design his own labyrinth and the other to try and reconstruct his opponent's maze. Each player can use thirty "walls," meaning he can blacken thirty sides of squares to form his labyrinth. Players cannot leave squares completely isolated.

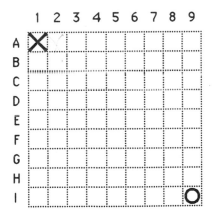

The starting point is the top left-hand square, A-1.

The player selects a direction and advances one square at a time until he decides to stop, finds a wall, or has moved five squares. On his next turn, he starts in the square where he stopped.

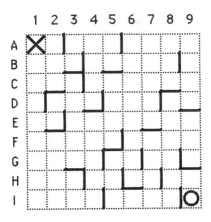

The winner is the first player to reach the bottom right-hand corner, I-9.

For example, Mark must explore the labyrinth in the illustration above. He decides to go towards the bottom and says, "I move from A-1 to B-1, to C-1, to D-1, to E-1, to F-1." After moving five squares, he stops. Now it is Paul's turn.

After Paul has moved, Mark moves again. "I go from F-1 to F-2, to F-3." He decides to stop, and Paul moves again.

After Paul has moved, it is Mark's turn again. "I go from F-3 to G-3, to H-3 . . ."

"Stop on G-3. There's a wall between G-3 and H-3," Paul interrupts. On the next turn, Mark starts on G-3.

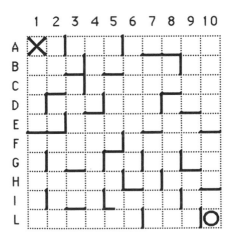

**Variations:** To make the game a little more difficult, the players may increase the number of walls.

The French use 10×10 playing boards with at least forty walls. They also move differently. A player selects a direction and advances one square at a time, until he finds a wall. On his next turn, the player can choose to start in any of the squares he crossed in the previous turn, including the starting square.

Here is an example of a French game: Pierre is exploring the labyrinth in the drawing below. On the first turn, he decides to go towards the bottom, and he starts moving, "From A-1 to B-1, to C-1, to D-1, to E-1 . . ."

"Stop on E-1!" says Victor. Pierre has found a wall. Victor plays his turn, and then it's back to Pierre again. He chooses where he wants to start among all the squares he crossed during his last turn, including the starting square (A-1, B-1, C-1, D-1, or E-1). He chooses C-1 and decides to move towards the right, "From C-1 to C-2, to C-3 . . ."

"Stop on C-3!" Victor interrupts.

# The English Labyrinth

*The gardens of many English castles have labyrinths, absolutely free from Minotaurs, but very beautiful and well cared for. Using paper and pencil, Queen Elizabeth's subjects play "labyrinth" in a more refined way, perhaps, than the rest of the world does.*

**Players:** Two

**Supplies:** Graph paper and two pencils

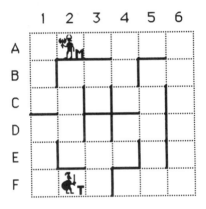

**Rules:** Each player draws two 6×6 playing boards. On one he designs his own maze; on the other, he tries to reconstruct his opponent's labyrinth. Each player marks a square with a T (for Theseus) and another with an M (for Minotaur). Each maze has twenty "walls," meaning each player can darken twenty sides of squares to make his labyrinth. Players cannot leave squares completely isolated. In addition, they cannot draw lines (straight or twisted) on more than three sides of any square. They can, however, build walls like those in square C-3 in the drawing below. The important thing is that from one end to the other, the wall cannot be longer than three squares.

Before the game begins, each player announces the starting and finish squares of his own maze so that his opponent can mark them.

On each turn, a player asks a question and then moves. The question involves asking if there is a wall between two adjacent squares. Players must always answer truthfully.

The move can consist of one, two, or three adjacent squares, starting in the one in which the player stopped on his previous turn. After the player announces his entire move, his opponent tells him if the move is possible or not. If it is possible, the player moves from his last position. If that is not possible, he tries again on the next turn. The first player to reach his opponent's finish square wins.

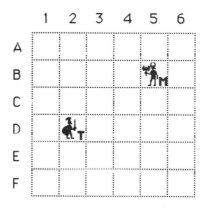

For example, Andy has designed the labyrinth above, and Kathy must explore it, starting on F-2 and finishing on A-2.

On her first turn, Kathy asks, "Is there a wall between F-2 and F-1?" Andy answers, "No." Kathy says, "I move from F-2 to F-1, to E-1, and then to D-1." Andy answers, "That's OK." Kathy is now on D-1, and it's Andy's turn.

On her second turn, Kathy asks, "Is there a wall between A-2 and A-1?" Andy answers, "No." Kathy says, "I move from D-1 to D-2, then to D-3, then to C-3." Andy answers, "No, stay where you are." He doesn't explain exactly where the wall is. Kathy stays on D-1, and it's Andy's turn.

On her third turn, Kathy asks, "Is there a wall between D-1 and C-1?" Andy answers, "Yes." Kathy says, "I move from D-1 to D-2."

Andy answers, "All right." Kathy is now on D-2, and it's Andy's turn. Notice that unlike *The Francoprussian Labyrinth,* the moves aren't necessarily straight.

**Variations:** The players may change the dimensions of the maze, the number of walls, and the rules for placing them.

They may also change the number and type of questions the players can ask. The players may decide to ask two questions per turn or to ask how many walls there are in a certain square. They may also decide to ask the questions first or to ask the questions after the moves. In our variation, the questions come before the moves.

# The Peruvian Mole

*J. H. Conway and M. S. Paterson invented* The Peruvian Mole *at Cambridge University in 1960 or in 1967 (historians disagree).*

**Players:** Two

**Supplies:** Paper and pencil

**Rules:** Draw three or more circles on a piece of paper. The first player connects two circles with a line and makes a circle in the middle of the line. Then it is the next player's turn. There are only two rules:

- A circle where three lines start is "full," and players cannot connect it with any others.
- The lines cannot intersect.

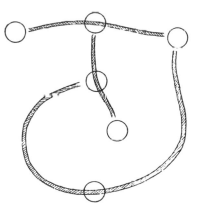

The winner is the player who forces his opponent into a position in which the opponent can no longer move.

Players may connect the circles drawn at the beginning, as long as they follow the rules. Obviously, this is not possible for the new circles, since a player has already connected them to two lines.

**Variations:** A variation of *The Peruvian Mole,* known as *Brussels Sprouts,* uses crosses instead of circles. Each stroke of the cross, called a "link," is the beginning of a line. This means that four lines rather than three can begin at each point. When drawing a new line, a player marks a dash in the middle of it, indicating the place for a cross with two opposite strokes still free.

Below is an example of a move. In the situation shown in the drawing on the left, the player connects the cross at the top left with the bottom and marks a dash in the middle of the new line. His move is illustrated in the drawing on the right.

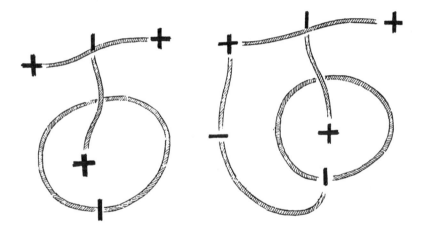

# Higher and Lower

Higher and Lower *is an extremely old game played by students.*

**Players:** Two

**Supplies:** Paper and pencil

**Rules:** The first player writes a number between 1 and 100 on a piece of paper. The second player must try to guess it by picking a number between 1 and 100. If he guesses the number, the round is over. Otherwise, if it is bigger than the secret number, the first players says, "Higher." If it is lower, he says, "Lower." The second player tries again to guess it.

The game continues until the second player guesses the first person's number. Then the players reverse roles and start with a new number. Whoever guesses his opponent's number in the fewest tries wins.

# Nim

Nim *is also known as* Marienbad *because we see it played in the film* Last Year at Marienbad. *This seems logical, although nobody dares to call the game* Dungeons & Dragons *"Extraterrestrial" just because we saw it played in the movie* E.T.

Nim *is very old and thought to be of Chinese origin, like spaghetti and gunpowder. And like the origins of spaghetti and gunpowder, this seems dubious as well. The name itself is derived from an Old English word meaning "to pilfer."*

**Players:** Two

**Supplies:** Paper and pencil

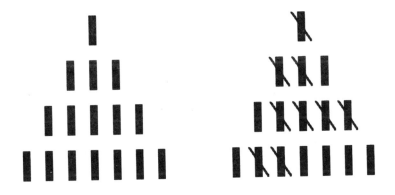

**Rules:** Before starting the game, the players draw various rows of vertical lines. The classical formation, like the one in the movie, has a row of seven lines, one of five, one of three, and one of one, as shown on the left. Another rather famous formation is the one with one row of three, one of four, and one of five lines. In fact, the players may decide on any number of rows formed by any number of lines. The concept of the game does not change.

The players take turns crossing out some of the lines. They can cross out as many as they want, as long as they are all in the same row. Whoever crosses out the last one wins the game.

**Variations:** Players may reverse the object of the game so that whoever crosses out the last line loses the game.

*Big Nim* is the "glutton" variation invented in 1910 by the American mathematician Eliakim H. Moore. The players pick a number before starting the game, for example, 3. This means that they can cross out as many lines as they want, as long as the lines are in no more than three different rows.

To play *Nimclock,* draw a certain number of lines (at least seven) to form a circle. The players take turns crossing out a line or two adjacent ones. Whoever crosses out the last one wins.

In a variation of *Nimclock,* the circle has twelve lines. The players can cross out from one to three adjacent lines per turn, but the top line (marked with the arrow below) must be the last one crossed out.

*Fibonacci Nim,* invented by Robert E. Gaskell, gets its name from Leonardo Pisano, called Fibonacci. He was the mathematician who introduced Arabic numbers to Europe in the third century.

In this variation, the first player crosses out as many circles as he wants, leaving at least one. Then the second player crosses out as many as he wants, as long as that number is not more than double the number crossed out by the first player.

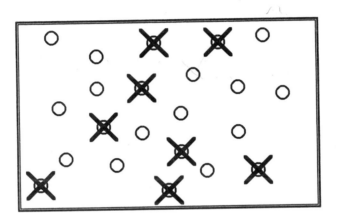

For example, at the start, there are twenty circles. Diane crosses out four, and sixteen are left. Jean can't cross out more than eight, so she decides to cross out five, leaving eleven. Diane can't cross out more than ten, so she crosses out one, leaving ten. Jean can't cross out more than two, so she crosses out exactly two, leaving eight. Diane crosses out two, leaving six. Jean crosses out one, leaving five. Diane crosses out one, leaving four. Jean crosses out one, leaving three. Diane crosses out one, leaving two. Jean crosses out the two circles that are left and wins.

# Nucleus

Nucleus *is a game published by Giorgio Cecchetti in the January 1983 issue of* Pergioco. *This Italian magazine also gave away a small cardboard playing board and a number of cards with the letters of the alphabet to help players with the game.*

**Players:** Two (or many, depending on the variation)

**Supplies:** Paper and pencil

**Rules:** Each player secretly writes six random words on a piece of paper. For example, he may write:

DEMOCRACY

RESPECT

ESTIMATE

PASSPORT

CREATIVITY

OFFICIAL

or,

WISDOM

FANTASTIC

TEACHER

URANIUM

EDUCATION

BLUNDER

The player divides the words into three parts: head, nucleus, and tail. Each of these three parts must contain at least two letters.

For example,

WI-SD-OM
FANT-AST-IC
TE-AC-HER
URA-NI-UM
EDU-CAT-ION
BLU-ND-ER

This paper is put aside. On another piece of paper, the player writes the six words, replacing all the letters of the head and tail with an equal number of dashes.

Next to them, he scrambles all the letters that compose the head and tail of the six words.

| | |
|---|---|
| --SD-- | IIIEEEE |
| ----AST-- | AAUUUU |
| --AC--- | OOTTWNN |
| ---NI-- | RRLDHBF |
| ---CAT--- | MMC |
| ---ND-- | |

The players exchange pieces of paper. Each player has five minutes to try to reconstruct the secret words written by his opponent.

When the time is up, they calculate the points. They count only the words they have recomposed, filling the blank spaces and using the letters given.

- For each word perfectly reconstructed, the player gets three points and his opponent loses three.
- For each reconstructed word that isn't exactly the opponent's word, neither player receives or loses points. This would happen for example, if instead of BLUNDER, the player had written FOUNDER or WOUNDED.
- For each unreconstructed word, the player loses five points, and his opponent wins five.
- For every letter left unused, the player loses a point, and the opponent wins one.

The game goes on to a new round.
The first player to reach a fixed number of points wins.


**Variations:** Because there is no way to predict how long a game will take, the players can have low scores and not reach the fixed number. When this happens, the players can agree to count only the positive points.

When playing *Nucleus* with more than two players, the players pass their papers to the player on their right the first time, the second turn to their left, the third turn to their right, and so on.

The players will need to change the scoring system.

- For each *unreconstructed* word, a player gets seven points.
- For each *reconstructed* word that isn't exactly the correct version, the player gets two points.
- For every word perfectly reconstructed, the player doesn't score any points, but the opponent who gave him the paper gets one point.
- For every letter left unused, the player gets one point.

Players exceeding 100 points are out of the game. The winner is the last player remaining in the game. If all players are out at the same time, the winner is the one with the lowest score.

# Regions

*Stephen Barr created this game, based on the use of four colors.*

**Players:** Two

**Supplies:** Paper and black, yellow, green, red, and blue pencils or one pencil as described in **Variations.**

**Rules:** On his first turn, the first player draws a zone on the paper with the black pencil. His opponent colors the zone with one of the other four colors. Then, using the black pencil, the second player draws another area, bordering the first one. The first player colors it and draws another zone, bordering at least on one of the other two zones. The game continues in this same manner.

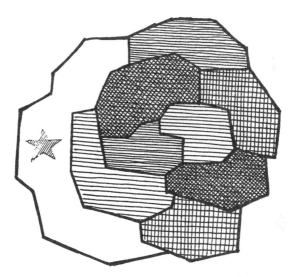

With each turn, the player waiting to color the area drawn by his opponent draws a new zone bordering on at least one existing zone. The only restriction is that a player can never use a color already used in one of the zones that border the zone he is about to color.

The loser is the player unable to color the zone drawn by his opponent because of this rule. In the drawing, the player must color the zone with the star, but he can't do this because it borders on zones that already have all four colors or, in this case, patterns. He has lost the game.

**Variations:** Instead of using color pencils, the players can fill in the interior with patterns, as shown in the drawing.

# Colors

*Created in 1971 by David L. Silvermann,* Colors *is a relative of* Regions.

**Players:** Two

**Supplies:** Paper and black, yellow, red, and blue pencils (or one pencil as described in **Variations**)

**Rules:** Start by drawing a random weave of curves, dividing the paper into regions. The players take turns, drawing one line, until the map has twenty to thirty regions, as shown below.

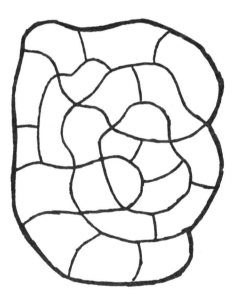

The game starts after the players draw the "map." Taking turns, the players color one of the blank zones in the map red, yellow, or blue.

The only restriction is that they cannot use a color already used in one of the bordering zones. The first player who cannot color a zone loses.

Zones must have more than one point in common to be considered bordering zones.

**Variations:** As with *Regions*, players may use only a black pencil to play.

Joseph and Lenore Scott have suggested a variation called *The Cartographer*. On a map like the one shown on the right, both players alternate coloring in regions. Each has a colored pencil and can only use that color. Players may not color a zone adjacent to one they already colored. The player who cannot color a zone loses the game.

# The Squared Map

*Published by Pietro Gorini in 1989,* The Squared Map *is a relative of* Regions and Colors.

**Players:** Two or four

**Supplies:** Graph paper and yellow, green, red, and blue pencils (or one pencil as described in **Variations**)

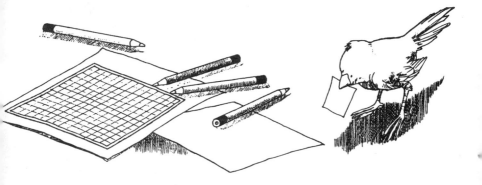

**Rules:** Draw a playing board that is at least 8×8 squares. The players have four colored pencils. Taking turns, they each color a blank square. If the square a player colors is adjacent (has a side or even only a corner in common) to one or more squares already colored with the same color, the player receives one penalty point per adjacent square of the same color.

The game ends when players have colored all the squares on the board. The winner is the player with the fewest penalty points. To play with boards that are larger or smaller, the number of squares must be divisible by the number of players.

**Variations:** As is the case with *Regions* and *Colors*, players may use only black pencils, substituting patterns for colors.

# The Track

*This is among the oldest of all paper-and-pencil games. Like many of the games in this book, it is more difficult to describe than to play.*

**Players:** Two or more

**Supplies:** Graph paper and different-colored pencils for each player

**Rules:** On a piece of graph paper, draw a track similar to the one below. It can be of variable width and length, but the more players there are, the wider it must be. Make sure it is clear whether the corners of the paper are part of the track or not.

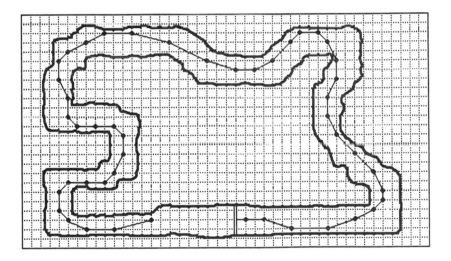

On the track, draw a line to represent both the start and the finish line. The line must be twice the length of the number of players. In the drawing above, only one person is playing.

Each player marks a circle where two lines intersect on the finish line. This represents his car. He cannot occupy the same spot as another car.

The players take turns moving. On the first turn, the player marks a dot on the corner of the square ahead of him. In the successive moves, he determines the "center of gravity" of the move, and he moves over it or to an adjacent corner.

To determine the center of gravity, he calculates the point at which his car will arrive if he moves it in the same direction and the same distance that he moved it the previous turn.

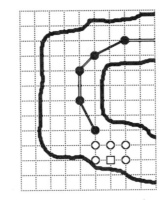

In the drawing above, for example, on the previous turn, the car moved following the diagonal of a rectangle of two squares per side. Its center of gravity will be on the corner marked with the white square or will be on the diagonal of a 2×1 rectangle oriented in the identical direction as the one in the previous turn. The player will be able to move on the same center of gravity or to one of the adjacent spots, marked with a white circle. The center of gravity can be out of the track.

The following rules apply when moving:

- On each turn, each car must move at least one square.
- The player has to link the circle marked on the previous move with the present one. The player connects both circles with a dash made with the pencil. No car may move in such a way that the line would cut or touch the edge of the track. If this happens, the car is "off the track."

- No car can move on a corner that does not belong to the track. If it has to do this, the car is off the track.
- No car may finish its turn on a corner already occupied by another car. No car's own track may pass over another car. In cases where the car must do this or go off the track, the player goes off the track.
- With each move, the player draws a segment on a series of squares or on the diagonal of a rectangle. However, cars can never move more than five consecutive sides or on the diagonal of a rectangle that has a side of more than five squares.

The penalty for a car that goes off the track is elimination from the game. The last car on the track wins the game immediately. Some people permit cars to return to the game after one, two, or even three missed turns. In this case, the car enters at the corner closest to the point where it left the track. The first move in the turn in which the car returns to the game may be only one square. On the next turn, it can move again, as determined by the center of gravity. Before the game starts, the players should decide which penalties to use.

In the unlikely event that a car can only move to a point already occupied by another car or can only move by running over another car, the player can move over the other car. If there are other cars on the segment, he has to choose the closest one. However, a car is out of the game when this occurs. In addition, the car that the player ran over is also out of the game.

Usually when cars run over other cars, too many cars are playing on a track that is too narrow. Of course, the other possibility is that a player is playing so well that his opponents can't anticipate his line.

The winner of the race is the first player to complete a lap of the track, crossing over the finish line. The other players have the right to complete their last turns, and, if any other cars cross the finish line, too, the winner is the player who crossed it with the largest number of squares. The other players still in the race may continue the game to determine their standings. If two or more players cross the finish line in the same turn, crossing it with the same number of squares, they tie.

The standings are important if you decide to make it a true championship.

**Variations:** The best-known variation of *Track* is actually simpler. The cars move only on the sides of the squares: one, two, three, or four sides per turn. They speed up or slow down a maximum of one square and turn a maximum of 90 degrees (they cannot turn backwards).

In another variation, the cars have no maximum speed limit and no center of gravity. However, they cannot increase or decrease their speed by more than one square. They cannot move along diagonals that have sides more than one square larger than the one in the previous turn. Cars may change directions by no more than 90 degrees if in the previous turn they had moved only one square.

The rules about finishing "off the track" and about crashes are the same.

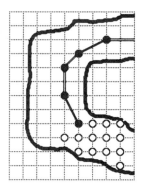

The drawing above shows the same turns made in the first version of the game on page 42, indicating the moves allowed by the rules in this version. As you can see, the car has at least thirteen places it can end its turn, versus the six it had in the first version. The new rules make it much easier to drive the car.

*Motocross* is another variation. The track includes marked obstacles (perpendicular cuts representing holes to jump and spots of difficult ground), which have to be cleared at precise speeds that are higher or lower than certain limits. In these areas, cars may not change directions or speed. Violating the restrictions established for an obstacle results in the same penalty as leaving the track.

Another interesting variation, developed at Leonardo Da Vinci High School in Genoa, Italy, uses simple moves on the sides of the squares. Cars may increase or decrease speed whenever they want. For example, the players can drive in first gear even if they were in fourth gear on the previous turn, and vice versa. The players, however, may only use each gear a limited number of times. Usually, players use a chart to keep track of the gears. Once a player has used his allotted number of turns in a gear, he cannot use that gear again. For example, a player cannot move more than ten times in third gear. The number of times will vary, depending on the dimensions of the track and the number of curves in the track.

# Synapse

*Pierre Berloquin, the inventor of the game, published the rules for* Synapse *in 1976.*

**Players:** Two

**Supplies:** Paper and pencil

**Rules:** Draw a 4×4 playing board of large squares. Each player starts with 25 points.

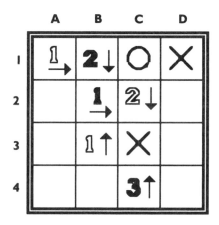

When it is his turn, a player writes a number between 1 and 3 in a square, subtracting that number of points from the amount he has available. He then draws an arrow towards the top, bottom, left, or right, indicating an empty square at a distance equal to the number he used in his square. His opponent must move to this square.

A player wins when his opponent cannot point to an empty square because it is not within reach or because he does not have enough points available.

The first player's initial move cannot be in one of the four central squares.

In the example game shown on page 46, Alice has started playing at the top left corner (A-1). Here is the rest of the sequence: Ellen B-1, Alice B-3, Ellen B-2, Alice C-2, and Ellen C-4. Alice must use C-1 (marked by the circle). She can do this by marking a 2 and pointing the arrow towards the bottom or by marking a 1 and pointing the arrow to the right. Ellen will have to use one of the two squares marked with an X.

# Sim

*The name of this game comes from its creator, Gustavus J. Simmons, who invented it in 1969. Others call it* The Hexagon Game.

**Players:** Two

**Supplies:** Paper and two pencils with different colors

**Rules:** Each player has a pencil with a different color. The players draw six dots in a circle. Taking turns, the players connect any two dots not yet connected.

The loser is the player who closes a triangle (drawn in his color) that includes three of the six dots.

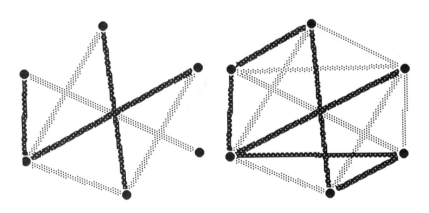

In the example shown on the right, the player with the darker pencil must move. He has three possibilities, but in each case he will complete a triangle of his color, losing the game.

# Black Box

*Eric Solomon invented* Black Box.

**Players:** Two

**Supplies:** Graph paper and two pencils

**Rules:** Prepare an 8×8 playing board.

Number it, counterclockwise from 1 to 32, starting at the top left, as shown below. One player, the Challenger, hides his board and marks four circles, or "atoms," on it in any four squares. His opponent, the Experimenter, must guess the position of the atoms by shooting "beams" into the Black Box and analyzing the effects.

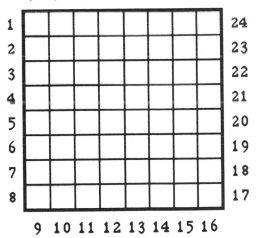

The Experimenter selects a number between 1 and 32, indicating a beam that crosses the board.

The Challenger follows its trajectory on his hidden board and tells the Experimenter if an atom has "absorbed" the beam or if it has left the board. If the beam goes off the board, the

Challenger announces the number through which the beam exited. Atoms detour or absorb beams according to the following rules:

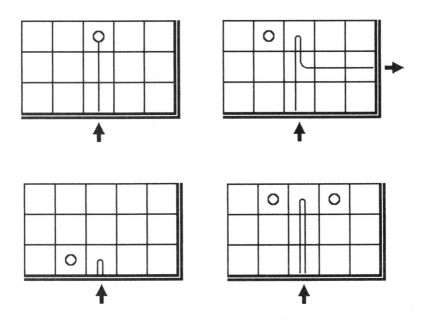

- An atom absorbs a beam that hits it, as shown in the top left drawing.
- A beam that would stop in or pass a square that is horizontally or vertically adjacent to an atom turns backwards one square and detours 90 degrees in the opposite direction, as shown in the top right drawing. When the beam turns backwards one square, it can end up off the board, as seen in the lower left drawing, finishing its trajectory on the same side of the board as it entered.
- If the beam stops in or passes a square between two atoms, as in the drawing on the lower right, it turns backwards, but it does not detour in a 90-degree angle because the atoms neutralize one another's effect.
- If none of these possibilities occur, the beam follows its trajectory and exits on the opposite side of the board.

The effects of the atoms on a beam accumulate along the trajectory of the beam until it exits the board or until an atom absorbs it. If the beam ends at an atom adjacent to another atom, the first atom absorbs it before the second can turn it back (see the beam at 6 in the drawing below). A beam detoured by one atom will detour again if it passes another atom.

Notice that all the trajectories of a beam could still be trajectories if you reverse the direction of the beam. If a beam enters the board at Point A and leaves at Point B, a beam entering at B must exit at A.

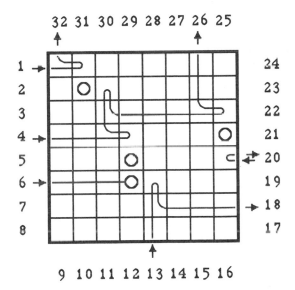

Here are some examples, using the board layout above. The beam entering at 1 must detour (according to the second rule) and exit at 32. The one entering at 4 detours three times (according to the same rule) and exits the board at 26. An atom absorbs the beam entering at 6 right away, before the atom at 5 could detour it to 11 (which would happen if the atom was not there). The beam entering at 13 detours to 18. The one entering at 20 exits at 20. A beam entering at 14 would exit at 27. If the top left atom were one square to the right, it would absorb the beam at 4 after it detoured towards the top.

The difficulty lies in the fact that the Challenger cannot tell the Experimenter where the beam detoured, how many times it detoured, or at which point an atom absorbed it. The only information the Challenger gives his opponent is when the beam left the board or whether an atom absorbed it.

The Experimenter writes down this information. If an atom absorbed the beam, he writes an A on the edge of the board next to the entrance point of the beam. If the beam exits at the same point it entered, he marks an R for reflected. If the beam exits at another point, the Experimenter marks the entrance point and uses a corresponding mark to indicate the exit point.

When he is ready, the Experimenter finishes the round by trying to identify the locations of the four atoms on the board. If he cannot do this, the round ends after a certain number of turns (for example, twenty).

Calculate the score for the Experimenter in negative numbers: one point per absorbed beam, one point per beam exiting at the exact same point it entered, and two points per beam exiting at a different point from where it entered. If the Experimenter has finished the game before the fixed number of turns, he earns a penalty of ten points per atom whose location he did not guess correctly.

After scoring the game, the players reverse roles and play another round. The player with the fewest penalty points wins.

**Variations:** Players may lower the penalty to five points for atoms the Experimenter cannot locate.

Expert players may want to use five atoms.

# Snake

*This is a new version of an old game.*

**Players:** Two

**Supplies:** Graph paper and a pencil

**Rules:** The first player is the Snake, and the second one is the Hunter. The Snake prepares a 6×6 playing board. Secretly, he selects six different numbers between 0 and 9, writing them in his own order. For example, he may use 1-2-8-0-4-3. Finally, he places the numbers in the six top-left squares of the board in either of the combinations illustrated below.

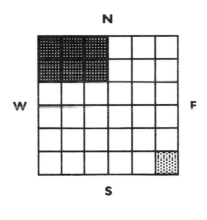

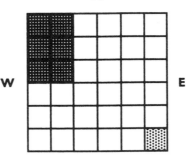

The player places the numbers in the order he thought of them. The first two numbers must be adjacent, and the second and third numbers must be adjacent, etc. The first number of the series is the "head" of the Snake. This must be in a square next to a blank one (it could not be where the 3 or the 8 is in the drawing on the left below).

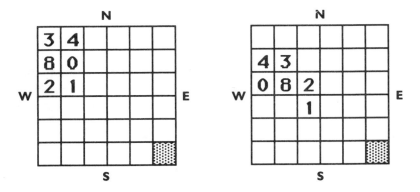

The Hunter starts the game by calling a direction. The Snake must respond with the numbers which are visible from that side of the board. The Snake must give the numbers in order, from left to right for the northern and southern sides, and from top to bottom for the eastern and western sides. In the starting position shown in the drawing on the left, the numbers 3 and 4 are visible from the north side, 4, 0, and 1 from the east, 2 and 1 from the south, and 3, 8, and 2 from the west.

Then the Snake moves his entire body two squares. The Snake may move horizontally or vertically but not diagonally. In the playing board layout on the right, the Snake from the drawing on the left has moved one square east and one square south. The whole series of numbers, the Snake's body, has moved. The head is now on the second square of the move. The next number in the series goes to the first square of the move, the third number in the square where the head was before, the fourth number in the square where the second one was, the fifth number where the third had been, and the sixth where the fourth was. The Snake erases the first set of numbers. The movement is very easy if you look carefully at the figures.

After the move, the Hunter calls a direction again and is told which numbers are visible from that side. In the board layout on the right, the numbers 4, 3, and 2 are visible from the north, 3, 2, and 1 from the east, 0, 8, and 1 from the south, and 4, 0, and 1 from the west. After answering the Hunter, the Snake moves again. After the Hunter receives the information, he tries to guess the series of six numbers.

Before moving, the Snake must tell the Hunter how many of the numbers match the ones in his series (same number in the same position of the sequence). If in the previous example, the Hunter says, "1-3-8-7-6-5," and the Snake answers, "Two numbers," because his series has 1 at the beginning and 8 in the third position. He does not say which numbers they are, nor does he say if the Hunter suggested the correct numbers in the wrong sequence.

The game ends when the Hunter guesses the Snake's series exactly or when the head of the Snake reaches the right-hand bottom square of the board (the grey one in the figure). The winning move of the Snake can be only one square if the head begins the turn adjacent to the ending square.

The players play two rounds, reversing their roles. If each wins a round, the winner is the player who has won his round in the fewest turns. If the number of turns is the same, the game ends in a tie.

**Variations:** To make the game harder for the Hunter, the Snake can use the same number more than once in his series.

The players can also decide that the Snake won't give the exact amount of numbers every time the Hunter guesses. Instead, the Snake will just say if he has matched any or not.

In a third and really wicked variation, the Snake can be a very poisonous cobra. The Hunter has only one try to guess the secret sequence of numbers, and if he fails, he loses the round. To make it easier for the Hunter, the Snake hides a six-letter word instead of six numbers.

# Squares

Squares *is a very popular game. In Italy, it is known as* The Battle of the Squares *or* The Hunt of the Fox. *The French call it* Pipopipette.

**Players:** Two

**Supplies:** Graph paper and pencil

**Rules:** On the graph paper, draw a rectangle with at least 100 squares. Taking turns, the players use a pencil to draw over one of the sides of a square. The player who completes a square, puts his initial or symbol in the center of the square and tries again. It is possible to complete many squares in the same turn.

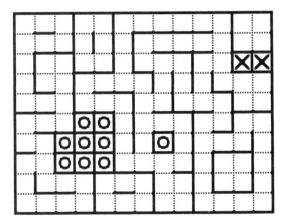

When the players have completed all the squares, they count their symbols or initials. The player with the most wins.

Players may consider the frame of the board as a completed side. A square on the side of the board needs only three more lines, and squares on corners need only two more lines.

**Variations:** Several variations use different types of boards, for example, the one shown below.

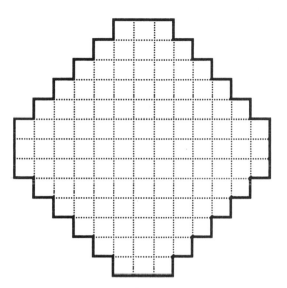

Some people consider the edge of the board as an unfinished side.

# Triangles

*This game is very similar to* Squares. *You can play it with a blank piece of paper instead of with graph paper.*

**Players:** Two

**Supplies:** Paper and pencil

**Rules:** Prepare a design of dots similar to the one in the drawing above. The design may be larger or smaller. Taking turns, the players connect two dots with a line. When a player closes a triangle (small ones only), he marks it with his initial or symbol and takes another turn. The player who closes the most triangles wins.

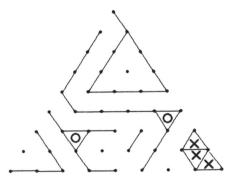

# Nazareno

Nazareno *is another relative of* Squares *with similar rules but an interesting twist. The name comes from the Nazareno Science High School in Rome, where students played it at the end of the 1970s.*

**Players:** Two

**Supplies:** Graph paper and pencil

**Rules:** Draw a rectangle of at least 100 squares. Taking turns, the players draw sides of the squares, using a straight line of any length they want. The important thing is that the line is straight and does not cover completed sides of the squares. Lines can cross other lines already drawn.

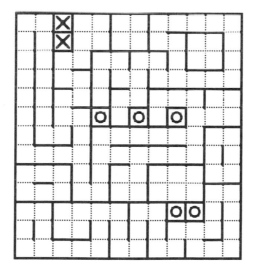

The player who completes a square draws his symbol or initial in it. It is possible to complete more than one square in the same turn.

When the players have completed all the squares, they count the symbols, and the one with the most symbols wins.

In this game, the edge of the board is considered to be a completed side.

Unlike *Squares*, players do not receive an extra turn when they complete a square.

# Triad

*This is a cousin of* Squares *and* Triangles.

**Players:** Two

**Supplies:** Graph paper and two pencils of different colors

**Rules:** The players take turns marking one side or one diagonal of a square on the graph paper. When they complete the perimeter of a triangle with their own lines, they earn as many points as there are squares in the area of the triangle. In other words, the whole perimeter of the triangle must be the player's color. In addition, the area of the triangle must be at least half of a square. Obviously, the same pencil line may complete more than one triangle at the same time. When this occurs, the score is the sum of the areas of all the triangles completed in that turn.

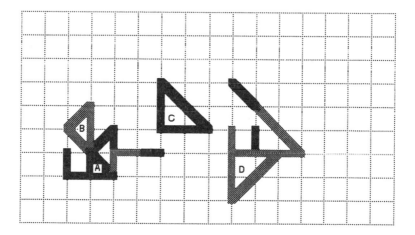

For example, in the diagram, Triangle A has an area of half a square and is worth half a point. Triangle B is worth one point. Triangles C and D are each worth 2 points.

The first player to reach thirty points wins.

# Fifty

*This game has infinite variations.*

**Players:** Two

**Supplies:** Paper and pencil

**Rules:** One player writes a number between 1 and 6 on the paper. His opponent adds a number between 1 and 6 to it and writes the total on the paper. The first player does the same, and so on. The player who reaches the number 50 wins.

**Variations:** The amount the players need to reach can vary as can the numbers played on each turn (for example, from 1 to 9). The objective of the game can be to avoid the target number or not to be the player who goes over the target number.

The *Game of the Matches* is very similar to *Fifty*. This game starts with seventeen matches on a desk or board. You can also draw seventeen sticks on a piece of paper. Taking turns, the players remove one to three matches (or cross out sticks on the paper). The player who takes the last match wins. This is possibly the most direct predecessor of *Nim*.

The rules can vary so that a player cannot remove the same number more than three times. You can also change the other rules or keep them so that you still play any number from 1 to 6, and the winner is the first to reach 50. His opponent can continue to remove that number as long as he does not use it more than three times.

In another variation, a player cannot use the same number more than twice.

# Word Hunt

*The name of the game implies enigmas, charades, and riddles. Although it is a simple game, it is stimulating.*

**Players:** Two or more

**Supplies:** Paper and pencil

**Rules:** Each player has his own piece of paper and must place himself so that no other player can see it. All players agree on a brief sentence or the name of a famous character. For example, "George Washington."

At a signal, the players write all the four-letter (or more) words they can find in the phrase. Foreign words and proper nouns are not acceptable. Players may use the singular or plural form of a noun, but not both. However, if a word is a noun and a verb, players may use it twice in different forms. In the example above, players may use the noun "rate" and the verb "rates." Players may not use "George" (proper noun), and they may not use the noun "ring" and the verb "ring." (They would have to use "ring" and "rings.") Players have a limited amount of time to find words.

To score the game, players begin by eliminating any word listed by every player. All remaining words are worth points. The score depends on the length of the word. A four-letter word is worth four points, a five-letter word is worth five points, a six-letter word is worth six points, and a word with seven or more letters is worth the number of letters plus one. The player with the most points after a certain number of rounds or length of time wins. Players may also decide that the first player to reach a certain score wins. This has to be agreed upon before the game starts.

**Variations:** If there are four or more players, the scoring system is different. A player loses points if he uses the same words as other players. The number of points lost depends on the number of players who used the same word. For example, a seven-letter word used by four players is worth $8-4=4$. There are no negative points, so a four-letter word written by five players is worth zero points, not minus one point.

# Verbal Rope

Verbal Rope *is somewhat similar to* Word Hunt.

**Players:** Two or more

**Supplies:** Paper and pencil

**Rules:** The first player spells a word with at least four letters and writes it on the paper. The second player has ten seconds to write another word with at least four letters.

- A player could use an anagram of the first word (SHOE—HOES) or a partial anagram (RESOLVE—LOVER) of the first word.
- A player can create the next word by changing one letter of the first word (WASH—CASH, PART—PANT).
- A player may simply change one syllable from the first word (TROUBLE—TROUSERS).
- A player may insert a core of one or more letters at the beginning of the first word (CARE—SCARE, TONE—ATONE), in the middle (CANE—CANDLE), or at the end (REAL—REALIZE).

Players may not use proper names. They may not reuse words already in the game.

A player who cannot find a word in ten seconds receives one penalty point. A player who writes an incorrect word also receives a penalty point.

When a player has a total of three penalty points, he is out of the game. The last player in the game wins.

# Havana

*This game is a version of* Hex.

**Players:** Two

**Supplies:** Paper and pencil

**Rules:** The game uses a board like the one shown below.

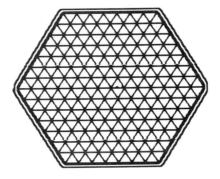

Taking turns, the players mark a circle on one of the intersections on the board. One player uses white circles, and the other uses black.

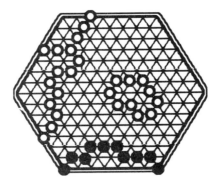

The winner is the first player to build one of the three configurations shown above wins:

- **A bridge.** This is a series of continuous circles joining two corners of the board, like the one with black circles at the lower edge of the game board shown at the bottom of the opposite page.
- **A ring.** This is a series of continuous circles containing at least one intersection of the board, like the one in the center of the figure formed by white circles.
- **A fork.** This is a series of continuous circles joining any three sides of the board, like the one on the left formed by white circles. The six intersections at the corners of the board cannot be a part of the sides of this combination.

# The Flat

*This is a very famous relative of* Tic Tac Toe, *also known as* The Game of the Five Crosses.

**Players:** Two

**Supplies:** Graph paper and pencil

**Rules:** Play on an area of graph paper as big as you like. One player uses Xs, and the other uses Os. Taking turns, they mark one of their own symbols on an intersection of the board.

Each time a player completes a line of five symbols, vertically, horizontally, or diagonally, he earns one point. The player connects the five symbols that compose this line with a pencil stroke so that no one uses them again.

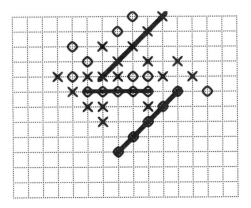

The player who has made more lines wins. The game can also end after a certain amount of time. In this case, the player with the most points wins.

**Variations:** One variation of this game consists of using the first and last symbol of a completed line to make other lines, as long as these symbols appear at the end of the new line.

The best variation consists of using any point of an existing line, as long as the two lines do not have more than one point in common.

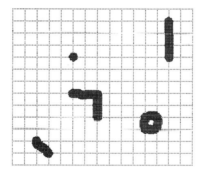

In another variation, the players create barriers at certain intersections on the board before the game begins, like the ones in the illustration above. No player may use these intersections. This makes the game more difficult.

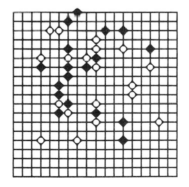

In a "Japanese" variation, based on the traditional game of *Go*, players mark intersections on a 19×19 line playing board, as shown above. A player who completes a line of five symbols wins.

Another variation, called *Ululo,* uses a board that can be as large as the players wish. The first player writes U, L, or O on a blank square. His opponent writes an A, M, or I. The first player wins if he completes the "word" ULULO, horizontally (from left to right or right to left), vertically (from top to bottom or bottom to top), or diagonally (in any direction). His opponent wins if he completes the "word" AMAMI, also in any direction.

In the example below, the first player has just won the game.

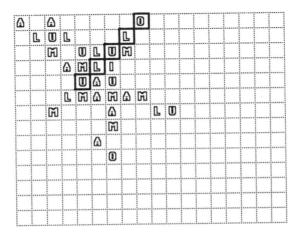

# The Big Snake

The Big Snake *is an example of a video game that you can play with pencil and paper.*

**Players:** Two

**Supplies:** Graph paper and pencil

**Rules:** The players delineate an area on a piece of graph paper in any shape and dimension they want. Each player selects one square as his starting point and marks it with his symbol.

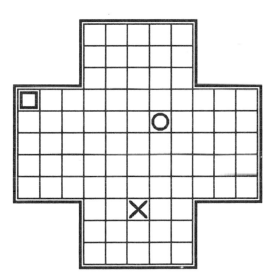

Taking turns, each player puts his symbol on a square that is adjacent to one side of the one he used in the preceding turn.

A player who is unable to move is out of the game. The last player in the game wins.

**Variations:** Before starting the game, the players blacken in some squares or groups of squares inside the area of the game, creating obstacles. The players cannot use these black boxes.

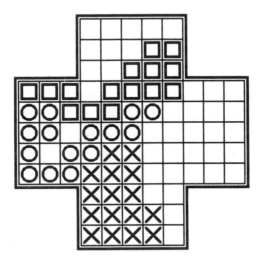

# Poe

*Sid Sackson invented this game.*

**Players:** Two

**Supplies:** Paper and pencil

**Rules:** After the players decide on a number (five is a good number), each player selects a secret word composed of that number of letters. The word may contain the same letter several times, or it may use five different letters.

Taking turns, the players choose a letter and ask a question. Typically, the first question each player asks is, "How many letters of your word are before the letter . . . ?" The opponent gives the number.

For example, Gloria's secret word is CARVE. Rose asks, "How many letters are before Q?" The answer is three, because CARVE contains three letters that precede the letter Q in the alphabet (A, C, and E). Notice that the letter chosen does not count.

The second question by each player in the next turn is typically, "How many letters of the word are between the letter . . . and the letter . . . ?" The third question might be, "How many letters of the word come after the letter . . . ?"

The fourth question is similar to the first one, the fifth one to the second, the sixth one to the third, the seventh again to the first and so on, until one player is ready to guess his opponent's word. In this case, the opponent has two possibilities. He can answer or refuse to answer. If he decides not to answer, the first player tries to guess the word. If he guesses it, he wins the game. If not, he loses. If the second player decides to answer, they both try to guess each other's words. If one gets it and the other one doesn't, the first one wins the game. If both guess it, the game is a tie.

# Numbers

*This is a very old game. British players call it* Bulls and Cows. *Italians know it as* Little Numbers *or* Strike and Ball. *Since 1972, players can buy it in a box-game version called* Mastermind.

**Players:** Two

**Supplies:** Paper and pencil

**Rules:** One of the two players writes a number with four different digits. For example, 3287 or 9301. His opponent, called the Decoder, must guess the number. He has an unlimited number of tries. On each try, he proposes a solution and receives useful information from his opponent. To do this, the Decoder writes a four-digit number on the paper, and the other player compares it with the one he wrote at the beginning of the game. For each correct digit in the correct order, he marks a + next to the number. He uses a − for each digit that is in the secret number but in a different position. The Decoder tries again, attempting to find the correct solution.

For example, Amy writes 3486. Liz tries to guess it by writing 2783. Amy writes " ± " next to the number. + is for the 8, correctly placed in third position, and − is for the 3, placed first instead of fourth. The Decoder has all the + and − responses for each try, but she does not know to which digits they refer.

When the Decoder duplicates her opponent's exact number, the round ends.

The players reverse their roles. They play one round each, and the winner is the player who guessed the number in fewer tries.

Before starting the game, the players must decide if the Decoder may use double, triple, or even quadruple numbers. If not, he will have to use numbers without repeating digits. Otherwise, he can use any four-digit number, for example 9339 or 0034. In both cases, the Decoder can use numbers that (because of information given by the first player) he knows are not the right numbers. In the previous example, Liz can play 3782, even if she knows that two digits in this number are incorrect.

**Variations:** In one version, each player receives as many penalty points as he had tries, and they play until one of the players reaches a predetermined number of penalty points, for example twelve. If this happens to the player who started the game by writing a number, he loses the game. If it happens to the other player, there is still one more round to be played so that each player has decoded the same amount of rounds. At the end of this round, the player with the fewest points wins.

The simplest variations involve changing the type of hidden code. The first variation changes the symbols. For example, the digits have to be between 1 and 5, or they can be any letter of the alphabet. The hidden code can include more letters or digits (five) or fewer letters or digits (three). The players may or may not restrict the code so that it cannot contain repeated elements.

A common variation consists of using a five-letter word. In this case, the Decoder must use real five-letter words to guess.

In the box game, the code uses colored pegs.

# Stymie

*David L. Silvermann invented* Stymie *in 1971.*

**Players:** Two

**Supplies:** Paper and pencil

**Rules:** The players draw a three-dimensional cube on a piece of paper. Taking turns, they mark a whole number between 1 and 8 on one of the corners. The players can only use each number once. The sum of the numbers on the same plane must be a prime number. The first player who is unable to move loses.

Remember that the prime numbers are 1, 3, 5, 7, 11, 13, 17, 19, 23, 29, 31, etc.

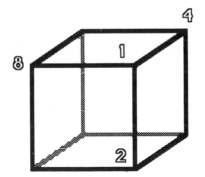

# Engel

*D. Engel invented this game in 1975.*

**Players:** Two

**Supplies:** Graph paper and pencil

**Rules:** Draw a 5 × 5 playing board. Taking turns, each player selects two squares in the same row or column and joins them with a line. The squares do not have to be next to each other. The squares do not have to be next to each other.

- New lines cannot intersect or create a T with existing ones. Lines can have common end points.
- Lines may not overlap existing ones.

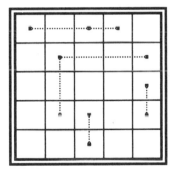

The game ends when one of the players cannot move. His opponent wins the game.

# Lasso

*Invented by Eric Solomon, this game takes its name from the lasso used in the American West to rope cows and horses.*

**Players:** Two

**Supplies:** Paper and pencil

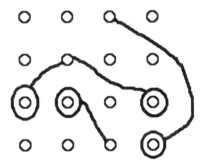

**Rules:** Draw a playing board of dots that is 3×3 or 4×4. Taking turns, the players draw a lasso, by starting on a dot, drawing a line, and then circling another dot. A player may not circle a dot that already has a circle or that is the starting point of another lasso. The lassos cannot intersect.

The first player who cannot draw a lasso loses the game.

# Horsey

*The original name of this game was* Blockades. *It used a board of hexagons that was more difficult to draw than this one.*

**Players:** Two

**Supplies:** Paper and pencil

**Rules:** Draw a playing board like the one shown on the left. One player uses black circles, and the other one uses white circles.

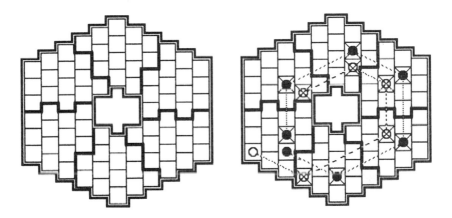

Taking turns, they mark their symbols on blank squares of the board. On the first turn, a player can place his symbol anywhere, but in future turns he has to place his symbol on a square on the same line as the last symbol placed by the other player, changing the direction clockwise by 60 degrees.

For example, in the playing board layout on the right, Black has started the game, and White is going to move. Every time they have moved, the players used an X to cross out the circle from the previous turn. This helps the players remember which circle is the last one.

To simplify things, the players can decide that one person will use numbers and his opponent will use letters.

The black rows divide the board into six segments, like the slices of a pie. These become important when counting the score. A player receives one point every time his opponent ends his turn in the same segment in which he started. When a player passes over one or more squares occupied by his opponent's circles, his opponent gets one point.

The first one to reach ten points, or the player whose opponent cannot move, wins.

# War of the Stars

*The basis for this game is the constant bidding war for stars—TV, movie, and sports stars.* War of the Stars *is the paper-and-pencil variation of the game known in England as* Footsteps. *A box game, called* Quo Vadis, *is also available.*

**Players:** Two

**Supplies:** Paper and pencil

**Rules:** Each player starts the game with $60 million and three stars, represented by three stick figures drawn on the paper. Taking turns, the players privately decide how much they want to bid for a star. The bids are between $1 million and all that they have. After they each write a bid, they both show the number at the same time and subtract it from their initial funds.

If a player has offered more than the other, he wins the star and draws a new man next to his stars. His opponent crosses out one of his. If both players have offered the same amount, neither of them gets the star. The players subtract their offer from their funds whether they win the star, lose a star, or the offer is a tie. If one player runs out of money, only the other one continues to bid. This means that this player can win by offering only $1 million. The game proceeds until one of the players runs out of stars, losing the game.

| BID | A—FUNDS AVAILABLE | BID | B—FUNDS AVAILABLE |
|-----|-------------------|-----|-------------------|
|     | 60                |     | 60                |
| 5   | 55                | 7   | 53                |
| 1   | 54                | 14  | 39                |
| 10  | 44                | 8   | 31                |

If both players run out of money before this happens, the player with more stars wins. If both players have the same amount of stars, the game ends in a tie. In the example illustrated, on the first turn, Player A offered $5 million, and Player B offered $7 million. Player A crosses out one star, and Player B adds one more. On the second turn, Player A offered $1 million, Player B offered $14 million. Player A crosses out one star, and Player B adds one more to his. On the third turn, Player A offered $10 million, and Player B offered $8 million. Player B crosses out one star, and Player A adds one.

**Variations:** Four players can divide into two teams. Two players become Team A, and the two others are Team B. Each of the four players starts the game with $60 million, and each can offer between $1 million and the total amount of money he has left. At the beginning, each team has three stars that belong to both players of the team.

To determine which team wins a star and which one loses a star, each team adds up their bids. The team that together has offered the highest amount wins the star. The other team loses a star. If one player runs out of money, his teammate proceeds to play on his own. The difficulty lies in the fact that teammates cannot consult to determine the amount to offer. They may only advise their teammates to "offer a lot," "offer a little," and so on, although this gives useful information to the opposite team, too.

Before the game starts, the players may agree privately on certain signals to communicate with their teammates. Both players can, for example, decide that touching the tip of the nose means to offer only $1 million or saying "bath" means to make a high offer.

# Wild Cats

*This game is very similar to* Tic Tac Toe, *but it is superior in two ways: Neither of the players has an advantage, and the loser can blame his loss on bad luck.*

**Players:** Two

**Supplies:** Paper and pencil

**Rules:** The players draw a 5 × 5 playing board, identifying each square with a letter and a number. One player uses X as a symbol, and the other uses O.

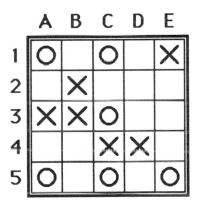

The objective of the game is to put four of the same symbols in a horizontal, vertical, or diagonal line. A player who does this wins the game.

On each turn, both players secretly write the coordinates of a blank square. At the same time, they both announce which one they have selected. If it is the same square, the turn ends in a stalemate and the game proceeds. Players may not select the same square they chose in the previous round.

If they pick different squares, each player marks his symbol on the square he selected, and the game continues.

The players are free to choose any blank square, except in one case. When one player has three symbols in a row and there is only one possibility of achieving the fourth symbol, he cannot choose that particular square. His opponent must select it.

# PART TWO
# STRATEGY

*"To find the exit of a labyrinth,"* said Guglielmo, *"there is only one way. At every new intersection you pass by, mark it three times. If you realize that you have already passed this way because of the marks on any of the paths, put only one sign. If all the passages have already been marked, it will be necessary to retrace your way back. However, if one or two passages are still without marks, choose one and mark it with two signs. When walking along a passage with only one sign, put two others next to it, so that now it has three. All parts of the labyrinth must be walked through and when arriving at an intersection, never take the passage with three signs, unless there is a passage without any signs."*

*"How do you know this? Are you an expert in labyrinths?"*

*"No, I am quoting an old text that I once read."*

*"And following this rule you can find the exit?"*

*"Almost never, but we can try."*

Umberto Eco (The Name of the Rose)

# BRIGITTE

First of all, note that in *Brigitte* a tie is not possible, which is also the case for *Hex*. One player always wins. Therefore, a winning strategy must exist. If the winning strategy were for the second player, there is nothing to prevent the first player from playing a meaningless first move. Once his opponent plays, the first player can play as if he were the "second player" to win.

Thus, the only winning strategy is for the first player, and it is only left to someone to discover it.

Oliver Gross is an expert on games theory. His winning scheme is shown. This is a board with thirty dots of each color. White moves first. If we rotated the board 90 degrees and changed the color of each dot, it would show the winning strategy for Black, whenever he moves first. The scheme is adaptable to boards of other dimensions.

In the drawing, White moves first, connecting the two bottom left dots. Black then plays, connecting two of his dots with a line that will have to cancel out a letter. White answers by marking the line that cancels out the same letter.

Notice Zs appear all around the edges of the board. Moving in these areas is useless. When Black moves on the edge, canceling out one of his Zs, White can move on any point of his own edge, canceling out a Z. He can also play on another letter. If the strategy says to play on a letter already canceled out, he will play on another letter instead.

# HIGHER AND LOWER

The most rational way to play is to use the procedure known as duality. First, try 50, then try 25 in case your opponent says, "High," or 75 if he says, "Low." Then 12, 37, 62, or 87. Depending on the answers, always choose the number that is exactly in the middle of the interval of the remaining answers. For instance, if you know that the hidden number is higher than 25 and lower than 50, play 37 or 38, the numbers exactly in the middle of 25 and 50.

Using this approach, you can guess the hidden number within a maximum of seven tries, the best guaranteed result.

Obviously, if your opponent knows this strategy, he can choose a number such as 49 or 26, so that if you use this strategy, it will take you longer to guess the number.

The rational player adapts his strategy to this possibility, using 11 instead of 12 and always trying the least likely numbers. Your opponent may count on this and choose more obvious numbers, such as 50 or 25. This can become a game of bluff and counterbluff. No one ever said that the most elaborate strategies lead to absolute victory.

# NIM

According to Charles Leonard Bouton, professor of mathematics at Harvard University around 1900, one player always has an infallible strategy. He based the name of this game on an Old English word meaning "to pilfer."

The strategy is based on the binary system, which is another way of writing numbers, using only 0 and 1. To find the binary representation of a number, divide it by 2 and write down the amount left over (0 or 1). Then divide the resulting "half" of the original number by 2 again and write the new remainder to the left of the previous remainder. Continue this process until the "half" will not divide in two, leaving a remainder of 0 or 1.

To win at *Nim,* the player must turn the number of sticks in each row into a binary number. The outlook is not good for the player who has to move when the total of each column is 0, or an even number. The outlook is good for a player who has to move when at least one column total is an odd number. Usually the outlook is good for the second player, if the player can cause problems for the first player by crossing out one stick in the last row.

## REGIONS

Mathematicians had a lot of trouble demonstrating the topological theorem of the four-color map, or Guthrie's conjecture. They formulated the problem in the nineteenth century: Given any geographical map, real or imaginary, how many colors do you need to cover all regions so that two adjacent regions would

not have the same color? The theorem states that four colors are sufficient.

Mathematicians made maps that required at least four colors. They proved that five colors were sufficient for any map, but they were unable to prove that four colors were sufficient, and, therefore, they couldn't prove the theorem. Neither were they able to prove the opposite: that there were maps requiring five colors—which would make the theorem false.

Finally in 1977, Kenneth Appel and Wolfgang Haken from the University of Illinois proved that the theorem is valid. To achieve this, they spent 1200 hours on a computer.

## SIM

Why does *Sim* use six starting points? Because if you had less, a symmetrical strategy would be possible, and the second player would never lose a game. For example, let's use five dots and call them AA, BC, DE, ED, and CB.

AA °

BC °               CB °

DE °        ED °

The first player begins by connecting DE with CB. We call this move DE-CB. The second player wins if he always makes a symmetrical move. The symmetrical move of DE-CB is BC-ED, reversing the letters.

If you define move BC-CB and move DE-ED as symmetrical, the defensive strategy of the second player is infallible.

With four dots (eliminating AA) the process is the same. However, with three dots or less, the game is meaningless.

Generally, the second player's symmetrical defensive strategy is possible when playing with a number of dots that is divisible by 4 or is divisible by 4 with a remainder of 1.

With six dots, a symmetrical strategy is not possible. You have to introduce a

sixth point, FF, and the move AA-FF does not have a symmetrical pair. It is also useless for the first player to make AA-FF his first move and then to play symmetrically in response to the second player's move. In doing so, he risks closing a triangle before his opponent does. In contrast to both *Hex* and *Brigitte*, making one more move is an advantage, not a disadvantage.

We can prove that the game will never end in a tie. Let's imagine that a certain game, once there are no more possible moves, ends in a tie. Having run out of moves, five lines must start at every dot. At least three of these must be of the same color.

Let's imagine that one of the players has a green pencil and the other a blue one. Green lines connect

Dots B, C, and D with Dot A. BC cannot be green or ABC would be entirely green. BC must be blue. The same reasoning applies to the segments CD and BD. They must also be blue. However, this is not possible, because that would form a BCD triangle entirely in blue, letting the green player win the game. Therefore, the initial hypothesis about the game ending in a tie is wrong. A tie is impossible.

## FIFTY

The strategy for the first player is simple. He has to write 1 the first time, 8 the second, 15 the third, 22 the fourth, and so on, increasing the total by 7 each turn until he reaches 50.

One of the players always has a winning strategy in each of the variations. To find it, he adds the minimum number allowed to the maximum, obtaining the amount, X. For example, if the numbers must be between 1 and 6, $X = 1 + 6 = 7$. Y is the total nec-essary to win. The player needs to calculate Y, $Y - X$, $Y - 2X$, $Y - 3X$, and so on, until he determines the lowest positive number possible. This is the first number he plays. If that number is lower than X, the first player can play it and win, using the numbers he calculated before. If that number equals X, the second player can add a number to arrive at X and win with the same system.

When playing the variation in which the player who reaches or goes over the total loses the game, the reasoning is exactly the same, except that the Y in the formula comes from the fixed total minus the lowest number allowed. In that case, $Y = 50 - 1 = 49$.

In the game with the matches, the same system could apply when $Y = 17$ and $X = 4$. The first player must, therefore, take one match, leaving sixteen on the board. On the next turn, he must leave twelve, then eight, and the fourth time four. The fifth turn, he wins the game.

## POE

When trying to discover the opponent's word, the questions "before" and "after" are equal. Asking, "How many letters are before F?" is the same as asking, "How many letters are after E?" The information is the same, considered from two different points of view.

It is difficult to say which is the better tactic. Initially, it is usually better to avoid wasting too much time trying to limit the letters to two, three, or four consecutive letters.

However, in selecting the secret word, the best tactic is to select one that has many anagrams. Your opponent can discover that you have used an A, E, L, S, and T, but he has no way to establish if you have written SLATE, STEAL, or LEAST. He will have to use some psychology, or more likely, try to guess it.

For experts, I suggest the following variations:

- A player can try to guess his opponent's hidden word by providing several possible solutions at the same time (a maximum of four) as long as each solution is an anagram of the others.
- Each game won when the second player decides not to answer is worth twelve points divided by the number of words that the first player offered as solutions.
- If the second player decides to answer, the eventual winner will get twelve points divided by the number of words he tried, multiplied by the number of words tried by his opponent.
- If both guess correctly, no one receives any points.
- The winner is the first player to reach fifty points.

To clarify, let's look at two examples.

Kathy and Andy have hidden words of five letters each. Kathy tries to guess, and Andy decides not to answer. Kathy suggests SHOOT and HOOTS. The hidden word is SHOOT. Kathy gets twelve points divided by 2 (the number of words she tried), making six points.

Sheila and Nancy have hidden five-letter words. Sheila tries to guess, and Nancy decides to answer. Sheila tries with RATED, TREAD, and DATER, while Nancy tries CLEAR and LACER. Nancy guesses it, and Sheila doesn't. Nancy gets twelve points divided by 2 (the number of words she tried), multiplied by 3 (the number of words that Sheila tried), for eighteen points. Had Sheila guessed it, no one would have received any points.

In another variation, the rules are the same, except that the players' guesses do not need to be anagrams of each other.

## STYMIE

In the basic game, the second player can always win in four moves. Let's analyze this simple tactic step by step.

On his first move, the first player will place a number on any vertex. If he has played an even number, the second player will play an odd number. If the first player has written an odd number, the second player will play an even number. The second player has to write this number on the face of the cube where the first player wrote his number, using the corner opposite the one used by the first player.

The basis of this tactic is that all prime numbers are odd numbers. Therefore, the two numbers at the ends of a face must add up to an odd number. One number must be even, and the other one must be odd, or the sum would be an even number. If an even number and an odd number appear on opposite corners of one face, the players cannot use the other two corners of that face.

The first player must then use one of the four corners of the opposite face. The second player will occupy the opposite corner of the same face, using an odd number if his opponent used an even number and vice versa, winning the game.

# Table of Games

| Title | Players | Paper | Colored Pencils | Difficulty |
|---|---|---|---|---|
| The Walls | 2 | Normal | No | * |
| Black | 2 | Graph | No | * |
| Mishmash | 2 | Normal | No | ** |
| Mine Field | 2 | Graph | No | * |
| Hex | 2 | Normal | No | ** |
| Brigitte | 2 | Normal | No | ** |
| Scaffold | 2 | Graph | 2 | * |
| The Francoprussian Labyrinth | 2 | Graph | No | ** |
| The English Labyrinth | 2 | Normal | No | ** |
| The Peruvian Mole | 2 | Normal | No | * |
| Higher and Lower | 2 | Normal | No | * |
| Nim | 2 | Normal | No | * |
| Nucleus | 2 or more | Normal | No | ** |
| Regions | 2 | Normal | 5 | * |
| Colors | 2 | Normal | 4 | * |
| The Squared Map | 2 or 4 | Normal | 4 | ** |
| The Track | 2 or more | Graph | 1 per player | *** |
| Synapse | 2 | Normal | No | ** |
| Sim | 2 | Normal | 2 | * |
| Black Box | 2 | Graph | No | *** |
| Snake | 2 | Graph | No | ** |
| Squares | 2 | Graph | No | * |
| Triangles | 2 | Normal | No | * |
| Nazareno | 2 | Graph | No | * |
| Triad | 2 | Graph | 2 | ** |
| Fifty | 2 | Normal | No | * |
| Word Hunt | 2 or more | Normal | No | * |
| Verbal Rope | 2 or more | Normal | No | ** |
| Havana | 2 | Normal | No | *** |
| The Flat | 2 | Graph | No | ** |
| The Big Snake | 2 or more | Graph | No | ** |
| Poe | 2 | Normal | No | ** |

# Table of Games (continued)

| Title | Players | Paper | Colored Pencils | Difficulty |
|---|---|---|---|---|
| Numbers | 2 | Normal | No | ** |
| Stymie | 2 | Normal | No | ** |
| Engel | 2 | Graph | No | ** |
| Lasso | 2 | Normal | No | * |
| Horsey | 2 | Normal | No | ** |
| War of the Stars | 2 or 4 | Normal | No | ** |
| Wild Cats | 2 | Normal | No | ** |

# Index

# Andrea Angiolino

Makes his living inventing games. In the past, he has written about stamp collecting, comics, music, old airplanes, and other trivialities. He has only one hobby: studying economics and commerce. Maybe one day he will become an expert in business computers. Meanwhile, attending college classes has turned him into an expert in paper-and-pencil games.

# Acknowledgments

For their help in researching and putting these games together, we would like to thank: Paolo Corsini, Enrico Colombini, Erica De Franceschi, Riccardo Del Frate, Tullio De Scordilli, Laura and Olivia Ercoli, Alessandro Gatti, Jon Johansson, Paola Lanciani, Pier Giorgio Paglia, Stefano Pischedda, Massimo Rega, Lina Maria and Lisbeth Sjostedt, Alessandro Vecchiarelli, and all our young friends from the Gattatico Public Library. Also thanks to Ennio Peres for his encouragement.

Special thanks to all my desk companions, from elementary school to the university, from Emilio C. to Valerio D. M. Without their fundamental contribution, I would never have written this book.